Rev Up Your Writing in Nonfiction Narratives

BY JULIA GARSTECKI • ILLUSTRATED BY MERNIE GALLAGHER-COLE

The Child's World®

Published by The Child's World®
1980 Lookout Drive • Mankato, MN 56003-1705
800-599-READ • www.childsworld.com

ACKNOWLEDGMENTS
The Child's World®: Mary Berendes, Publishing Director
Red Line Editorial: Editorial direction and production
The Design Lab: Design

PHOTOGRAPHS ©: Michal Bednarek/Shutterstock Images,
6; Sergey Novikov/Shutterstock Images, 12; Darrin
Henry/Shutterstock Images, 18

ISBN 9781634070652
LCCN 2014959944

Printed in the United States of America
Mankato, MN
July, 2015
PA02261

ABOUT THE AUTHOR

When Julia Garstecki was in elementary school, she loved writing reports and stories. She did not realize she was writing nonfiction narratives. It is still her favorite thing to write.

ABOUT THE ILLUSTRATOR

Mernie Gallagher-Cole is a children's book illustrator living in West Chester, Pennsylvania. She loves drawing every day. Her illustrations can also be found on greeting cards, puzzles, e-books, and educational apps.

Table of Contents

CHAPTER ONE

What Is a Nonfiction Narrative?

Have you ever read a **biography**? How about a book about a famous event? If so, then you have read a nonfiction narrative. A **narrative** is a story. **Nonfiction** is writing about real events. So, a nonfiction narrative is a story about real events.

Newspapers are nonfiction texts. But they give important **details** right away. Nonfiction narratives give details in a different order. These narratives take the reader on a journey. There is a beginning, a middle, and an end.

A biography is a nonfiction narrative. It tells a person's life story. A nature book about an animal's life cycle is a nonfiction narrative, too. It tells how the animal was born. Then it explains how the animal changes as it grows.

Start your story by brainstorming. Think about where you can find information. Then collect as many facts as you can. You can sort through the details later. You might not use all the details you collect.

You can use three Rs to help you write your story. The first R is *research*. The second is *real-world information*. The third is *review*.

First, research your topic. Letters, newspapers, and books are good sources. The more **current** your source

Nonfiction narratives cannot be made up. They must be true. For example, you should not write that a zebra and a lion are friends. That would not happen.

is, the better. That means your information should be as new as possible.

Finding real-world information means getting the right details. Try to visit the **setting** of your text. If you can, talk to the person you are writing about. You can also interview other people who know the person. Find someone who saw the event.

Sometimes you cannot travel to the setting of your story. Or you cannot speak to the people in your text. You can do other things, though. Find pictures of your setting. Look for quotes in articles and books. For example, suppose your topic is the Pilgrims. You will not find a living witness. But many experts would be happy to talk about what they know. You can e-mail or call them.

When you review your story, you should check your sources. Look for different books that give the same information. This will help you make sure the information is true.

CODE TALKERS

Places where I can get information

Native American museum

Internet

- Interviews of code talkers
- Military Web sites that explain code talkers
- Native American Web sites

Library

- Books
- DVDs
- Old newspapers

Interview military veterans and experts

Notes about code talkers

Focus on how they started and how they helped.

Enemies learned what the United States

was doing in World War I.

Army needed better codes.

Code talkers helped the United

States win wars.

QUESTIONS
What are some resources the writer will use?
What are some details the writer will include?

Native Americans spoke different languages.

Choctaw soldiers spoke about battle plans in their language.

Army generals realized no one could understand their words.

Choctaw were placed in different battle areas.

They began a training program.

It was top secret.

CHAPTER TWO

Writing the Story

Y ou are done brainstorming. Now it is time to start writing. Remember, a nonfiction narrative reads like a story. That means it should have characters and a plot. It should also have a setting and **dialogue**.

Decide who or what your story is about. Characters are the subject of your text. The subject is usually a person or an animal. But it could also be a place or an event. It could even be a plant. The subject can be anything that changes over time.

Plotting means putting your story in order. Before writing, think about what you are teaching your readers. Where should your narrative start? When should it end? Nonfiction narratives usually go in **chronological** order.

The setting is where and when your story takes place. The setting affects your characters. For example, animals use their setting as shelter. If writing about the past, you

Using dialogue can be tricky. You must find quotes that people actually said. These quotes should come from written sources. Do not make them up.

must know what was possible at the time. For example, Pilgrims traveled to America by ship. They could never travel by plane. How did this affect their journey?

Biographies are fun nonfiction narrative pieces to write. They usually start when the subject was young. So, ask yourself questions. What was her childhood like? What did she do? How did she do it? Then, describe the person at different ages. Think about what made her important.

A biography also needs a good ending. This should explain how the person affected the lives of other people. Also, talk about whether the person has died or is still living. If she is alive, what is she doing now?

THE FIRST CODE TALKERS

In 1918, the United States was fighting Germany in World War I. The US Army was having a hard time. The Germans seemed to know what the US Army was going to do. This put American soldiers in danger. The army needed a way to keep its plans secret. Then the soldiers would be safer.

Some Native Americans were in the US Army. Choctaw soldiers often spoke to each other in their own language. Nobody else could understand them. That gave the generals an idea. If other American soldiers could not understand the language, the Germans would not be able to either.

The generals used the Choctaw language as their code. The Choctaw soldiers were now called code talkers. They were placed in different army units. They used special phones to call each other. If the Germans were listening, they would not understand. Then the code talkers would hang up and tell the soldiers in English what to do.

QUESTIONS
What facts did you learn about code talkers? What makes this passage sound like a story?

CHAPTER THREE

The Story in Science

Have you ever written about a science experiment? You probably had to explain your materials and procedure. Then you wrote about your results. In nonfiction narratives, you might write some of that. But there is a story behind every scientific discovery. In nonfiction narratives, that story is the focus.

Consider writing about a new discovery. Maybe the discovery was an accident. Did a mistake lead to new information? Who was involved? What did they do? Learn what problems the scientists had along the way. Your readers might forget about specific details. But they will remember how the scientists developed something.

Revising is very important. It makes your writing better. If possible, put the story away for a while. Reread it again after a few days. This will help you catch mistakes.

Perhaps you are assigned a topic you do not like. But with nonfiction narratives, you get to find the story. Keep an open mind. You will probably learn some interesting facts!

When you reread your piece, read it from beginning to end. Make notes where things do not sound right. Also, look to see if anything needs more explanation. You might have to do more research. Maybe you forgot to mention an important part of the subject's life. Sometimes, a sentence needs to go somewhere else in the story.

Other times, a sentence may be hard to understand. In that case, rewrite the sentence using different words.

Writing your piece will be fun if you like your topic. So, what do you want to learn about? Start researching. Once you have some facts to work with, it is time to begin writing!

THE HISTORY OF ELECTRONIC GAMES

One of the first electronic games made was in 1940. A scientist made a machine called Nimatron. It played a game called Nim. Thousands of people lined up to play at the World's Fair. Most people had never seen a game played on a machine. They thought it was very exciting. The machine won most of the games it played.

In the 1950s, people built a computer that could play chess. This computer was very big. It took up an entire room. A human chess expert played the computer. The human won easily. But he said the computer was not bad.

In 1961, college students created a video game called *Spacewar*. Players saw two spaceships on a screen. The goal was to blow up the other player's ship. This video game was one of the first that used controllers.

QUESTIONS
What is the plot?
How do you know this story is a nonfiction narrative?

TIPS FOR YOUNG WRITERS

1. The more nonfiction narratives you read, the better you will write.

2. Keep a notebook with ideas that interest you.

3. When you read about an event in the newspaper, think about what the article is not telling you. What else could you find out?

4. Who is your favorite movie star? What can you learn about him or her? Write a biography.

5. Interview friends and family to learn more about them.

6. When you interview people, ask open-ended questions that begin with *why* and *how*.

7. When you visit different places, take lots of pictures. Notice details that you can include in your writing.

8. Knowing what to include in your narrative can be hard. Think about what must be told so the whole story makes sense. Sometimes you have to take out information you like because it does not help your story.

GLOSSARY

biography *(bye-AH-gruh-fee)*: A biography is a book about a real person. I read a biography about George Washington to learn more about him.

chronological *(KRAH-nuh-LAH-ji-kuhl)*: Chronological means in the order that things happen. I described my day in chronological order, so I started with when I woke up and finished with when I went to bed.

current *(KUR-uhnt)*: Current means recent. The newspaper from this morning is the most current information.

details *(DEE-taylz)*: Details are pieces of information. Two details helped catch the robber: he was wearing purple socks and a red hat.

dialogue *(DYE-uh-lawg)*: Dialogue is a conversation between two people. The dialogue in the book helped us learn what the characters were thinking.

narrative *(NAR-uh-tiv)*: A narrative is a story. Grandma told me a narrative of when she came to the United States.

nonfiction *(non-FIK-shun)*: Nonfiction is information based on real events. Science books are nonfiction.

plot *(PLOT)*: A plot is what happens in a story. The movie had a simple plot: a boy found a map and searched for treasure.

research *(ri-SURCH)*: Research means to investigate and study an event. Before I started writing about turtles, I had to go to the library to research them.

revising *(ri-VIZE-ing)*: Revising means making corrections or edits to a piece of writing. After writing a first draft, the author started revising the text.

setting *(SET-ing)*: A setting is the place where an event happens. The setting for my piece is in the jungle.

TO LEARN MORE

BOOKS

Benke, Karen. *Rip the Page!: Adventures in Creative Writing*. Boston: Roost Books, 2010.

Mazer, Anne, and Ellen Potter. *Spilling Ink: A Young Writer's Handbook*. New York: Roaring Book Press, 2010.

Minden, Cecilia, and Kate Roth. *How to Write an Interview*. Ann Arbor, MI: Cherry Lake Publishing, 2011.

ON THE WEB

Visit our Web site for lots of links about nonfiction narratives:
www.childsworld.com/links

Note to Parents, Teachers, and Librarians: We routinely check our Web links to make sure they're safe, active sites—so encourage your readers to check them out!

INDEX